B. WILSON

COVER YOUR **TRACKS**
WITHOUT CHANGING YOUR IDENTITY

How to Disappear Until You **WANT** to Be Found

Paladin Press • Boulder, Colorado

Other books by B. Wilson:
Backyard Catapults: How to Build Your Own
How to Get Rich as a Televangelist or Faith Healer
Under the Table and Into Your Pocket:
    The How and Why of The Underground Economy

Cover Your Tracks without Changing Your Identity:
How to Disappear Until You WANT to Be Found
by B. Wilson

Copyright © 2003 by B. Wilson

ISBN 13: 978-1-58160-419-1
Printed in the United States of America

Published by Paladin Press, a division of
Paladin Enterprises, Inc.,
Gunbarrel Tech Center
7077 Winchester Circle
Boulder, Colorado 80301 USA
+1.303.443.7250

Direct inquiries and/or orders to the above address.

PALADIN, PALADIN PRESS, and the "horse head" design
are trademarks belonging to Paladin Enterprises and
registered in United States Patent and Trademark Office.

Visit our website at www.paladin-press.com

Contents

Preface

The human condition being what it is, dreaming of a better life is a pastime most of us indulge in at least occasionally. One of the most common fantasies is that of disappearing completely and leaving undesirable circumstances behind. Many who dream of this have severe financial or personal problems that have made their present lives intolerable. Numerous books have been written over the past 30 years showing these readers how they can shed their old identities and start over. These works have helped thousands to escape unpleasant and often dangerous situations and literally make a fresh start.

As valuable as these books are, however, they have one common limitation. They assume that the reader wants to make a total and permanent change, and the instructions they offer are given with that assumption in mind. For many, however, this is simply not the case. They want or need to get away but do not wish to permanently sever ties to their old life. What they need is a way to escape for a few weeks or months, perhaps up to a year; get some breathing room from their problems; and then decide what their next step will be. The usual "change your identity" books are not suitable for them. It is for these people that this book was written.

I have been in such a situation myself. The year 2001 was traumatic for me personally, and I realized one day that I had to get away for a while. I also knew that people like creditors and maniacal former significant others, as well as well-meaning but nosy friends, would want to keep tabs on me. This was unacceptable. So I developed a plan for disappearing one day and leaving no tracks that one could follow to find me.

I also knew, however, that I did not want to stay away forever. I could not stay goodbye to Dixie permanently, being a native of the South and a lover of the region. Nor did I wish to sever all contact with family and friends. I was not wanted by the law or the Mob. What I needed was a "light identity change," one that would safely shield me from snoops for several months while I cleared my head and figured out my next move.

I was able to accomplish this with complete success. I found a sanctuary where I could stay long-term and be treated well. I made a plan, saved my money, and reduced my possessions to a minimal level. Then one day I quite literally just took off, driving to another region of the country where friends awaited to offer me shelter, aid, and assistance. I established red herrings and false clues to mislead others as to my whereabouts. While in the new area, I established employment and a savings account without changing my Social Security number. I kept a fairly low profile but was by no means a hermit. I traveled widely across the state I lived in, enjoying its sites and attractions openly. As I suspected, there were those who tried to find me, but they were unsuccessful. When my self-imposed "sabbatical" was nearing an end, I sat down to write this book as I prepared to return to the South and pick my life back up.

Now you can learn how I covered my tracks without changing my identity. This book is based upon my own experiences, as well as research and discussion with others who have gotten away for a while and were not found. If you believe that you could do with a little time out, then read on and learn how you too can take a vacation from your regular life for a while.

Introduction

What is going on in your life right now? Have things taken a downward turn for you? Are your finances in a mess? Are you in a relationship, or even a marriage, that is in bad shape? Do you hate your job? Feeling mean, nasty, and tired? Well, don't go postal, don't get intoxicated, and don't send your money to a television evangelist.

Get out.

Rarely in difficult circumstances does one have the presence of mind to calmly and rationally evaluate the situation and decide on a course of action. Emotional stress; pressure from associates, family, and friends; and false feelings of guilt or misplaced loyalty can all hinder clear thinking. The best thing to do is get away, even if it is just for a day or two, and let yourself calm down. Put some distance between you and your problems, and very often solutions will come to you that you never would have thought of otherwise.

Getting away almost always helps, but the critical question is, "For how long?" For what amount of time should you stay away before returning to tackle your situation? For that matter, *should* you return? Tenacity is not always a virtue.

In some cases, such as where you are in extreme danger from a murderous and relentless foe, a permanent escape may be best. This will require a heavy-duty new identity, with all ties to your past life erased. In many other cases, though, leaving permanently may do more harm than good. Factors to be considered include your reasons for leaving, probability or desirability of being able to return to your old life, ability to cope with living a new life, and the diligence and resources of your potential pursuers.

Let's look at some hypothetical scenarios and see if we can figure out the best thing to do in each one.

UNLUCKY IN LOVE LARRY

Larry Jones is a married man, 32 years old, with a decent job that he tolerates but doesn't really like. His health is good, his credit fair, and he has no kids. He is a law-abiding, tax-paying citizen with a modest home he owns and a few thousand dollars in the bank. He lives in Atlanta, Georgia. He has always dreamed of hiking the entire Appalachian Trail, which begins in the northern part of the state. But he could never get the time off for the five to six months the adventure would require.

Larry's biggest source of both joy and sorrow is his wife Darlene. A moody, demanding woman, she frequently torments him with verbal abuse and nagging. When she is nice she makes him quite happy, but her niceness usually depends on her having her own way. When Larry does not give her what she wants she becomes angry and contrary, either berating him or trying to make him feel guilty. Larry loves Darlene but is afraid to think of spending the rest of his life with her.

One day Larry is on his way home from work. He has been upset all day because of a fight he and Darlene had that morning. He decides to stop at the florist and buy her a bouquet of roses; maybe that will smooth things over and he can have a peaceful evening for a change.

When he pulls into the driveway he notices the lights are out. He got off an hour early from work but did not call home because he wanted to surprise Darlene. There is a red sports car he has never seen before parked next to Darlene's Ford Escort, which he bought for her last birthday. He steps quietly in the house, afraid his wife is not feeling well and not wanting to wake her. Strange noises from the bedroom grab his attention, and he tiptoes toward it. The door is slightly ajar, and he sees inside. Darlene is on her knees giving oral pleasure to another man. The act is clearly voluntarily, and both she and her partner are enjoying it immensely.

Larry never dreamed Darlene could be unfaithful, and the sight is too much for him. He drops the flowers he bought and runs from the house, getting in his car. His wife pursues him and bursts outside in her bathrobe, ordering him to stop as he pulls out of the driveway. He hears her cursing loudly as he speeds away.

Larry cruises the city streets aimlessly until late in the night, trying to decide what to do. He is afraid to go home; he knows that his patience with Darlene is over forever and feels he is likely to hurt or even kill her if he sees her again. He glances down at the briefcase on the passenger seat beside him and remembers that he has a presentation to do the next day at work that he has not even begun to prepare for. The consequences from his overbearing boss will be severe if he is not ready to do it. He sees a sign for Interstate 75, which can have him in the mountains in less than two hours. It is early March, and warm weather will soon blanket the state. He sees the chance to do something he has always dreamt of: shuck conventional responsibility and the burden of debt and live as a free spirit.

This will of course mean the end of his good credit and his stability, but he honestly doesn't care. He has met others who have lived as nomads for years, and though they had difficulty eventually readjusting to society, they nonetheless had stories to tell that would make their grandchildren roll their eyes in wonderment. In fact, Larry has fantasized about completely changing his identity and adopting a new life altogether but would like to test the waters by disappearing for a limited time first.

What should he do?

WORKING MAN JACK

Jack Bradley is a self-employed carpenter. His prize possession is a pickup truck that he uses in his trade. Besides carrying his tools and hauling work-related loads, it serves as his only means of transportation. He purchased it a year ago when he was working 50 to 60 hours a week at an excellent hourly wage. The payments are more than $500 a month. At the time he bought the truck, Jack could easily afford the note. He was living with his mother for free and bringing home almost a thousand dollars a week. But his mom has since moved to a nursing home, and her house was sold to meet the expenses, so Jack is now renting. His work slowed down, and he is currently earning half of what he was 12 months ago. As a result, he is several months behind on his payments, and the finance company has become very threatening. Jack is afraid to declare bankruptcy, knowing it will destroy what is left of his credit.

One night he is talking with his brother, who lives in another part of the state. He mentions that there is a great deal of construction going on in his area, and carpenters are in high demand at excellent wages. He offers to let Jack stay with him while he seeks employment in the area.

There is only one problem: the finance company sent Jack a certified letter the previous day. If he does not bring his payments up to date within seven days, his truck will be repossessed. The amount now due is over $2,000. Jack wants to pay his bills but cannot raise the lump sum in a week. What should he do?

SALLY AND HER STALKER

Sally Jones is a 20-year-old single mother with a 2-year-old daughter. She has been living with her new boyfriend for several months. At first he was very kind and loving to both her and her child, and she thought she had met Mr. Perfect. But lately he has become verbally and physically abusive. She has also discovered that he has a substance abuse disorder and spent time in prison for felony assault. One evening he comes home drunk and beats her severely. She flees to her mother's home with her daughter and calls the police.

The boyfriend is soon arrested, and she decides to press charges. He responds by showing up at the mother's house that weekend after making bond, waving a gun and threatening their lives.

The law shows up and takes him away, and Sally has a restraining order put on him. But she fears that he will disobey the order and come after her again. She is assured by her attorney that, because of the prior conviction laws in her state, Jack faces a minimum of 20 years in prison. But his trial date is several months away, and for now he is out on bail. Sally is terrified for herself and her daughter. What should she do?

* * *

In each of the above scenarios we met people whose lives have taken serious downturns because of circumstances outside their control. In each case there is little or nothing they can do by sticking around and trying to "fix" things. If Larry goes home to his wife he will likely assault her, or he will be assaulted by her and/or her lover. He also knows his marriage is beyond repair but does not have the emotional strength to deal with a divorce at the current time. As for Jack, it is very unlikely that his creditors will work out a payment plan with him, and he will lose the ability to support himself if his truck is repossessed. In Sally's case, staying in her local area puts her life, as well as that of her daughter, at risk. In all of these situations, the main characters would benefit enormously by covering their tracks and disappearing for a while.

Traditional new identity methods could be of assistance to these people, but they would entail a heavy cost indeed. If Larry does not eventually deal with his situation, his wife can claim abandonment and obtain a divorce with terms favorable to her, getting the house and other assets. Jack could slip away, change his critical identifiers, and find work under a new ID, but his financial resources are limited and he is dependent upon his vehicle. In Sally's case, she will be safe if she can only survive long enough to see her stalker imprisoned.

Completely dumping one's old life and starting fresh has consequences that many people cannot or will not deal with. Besides the time and effort involved in changing data such as one's birth date and Social Security number, there are the challenges of establishing a complete new identity from scratch— severing old ties to friends, work, and family permanently and adapting to a new location and new habits. One recent guide to "disappearing" lists almost 20 pages of "do-nots" and other instructions for the disappearee! Among the things urged: don't go to church, don't ever play your stereo too loud, don't travel cross-country by bus, let life insurance policies lapse, be careful to always dress in a very low-key manner, surrender any claim to refunds from utility companies when you discontinue their services, don't have milk or other products delivered to your door, don't join political organizations, don't work on your car in your yard, don't get to know your neighbors, don't express controversial opinions, and the list goes on and on. How many people could endure such a restrictive existence year in and year out? In all but the most severe cases, complete and permanent identity change carries a price too high to pay.

On the other hand, the average person can put up with all sorts of inconveniences on a temporary basis. In my own case, I could never endure the regimen dictated above for any length of time. However, I was able to tolerate many things, including unfamiliarity with the region and working at less-than-ideal employment at first, as well as more minor irritants such as higher prices and lots of pollen. The benefits of escaping my old situation for a while more than outweighed the transitory setbacks. Since I knew that I would eventually return to the South, my patience held, though it was at times taxed. I was even able to make a few new friends and tell them I am a writer (since my true profession, "wandering miscreant," doesn't look too impressive on the ol' resumé).

To summarize: There are many situations in which leaving the scene for a while can be the best thing to do. At the same time, most people probably do not need a complete identity change, just a way to be "invisible" for a few weeks, maybe several months, while they get their head straightened out and wait for things to settle down back home. This can be accomplished by establishing a "new ID lite." The techniques for doing so are described in detail in the rest of the book.

A final word: since no two people's situations are identical, I have avoided describing a "one size fits all" method in the following chapters. Covering one's tracks can be accomplished in a multitude of ways, and what is best for one person may be completely inappropriate for another. What I offer instead is a "buffet" of ideas and suggestions that readers can use to tailor their own solution to their problems. Use what works for you. Now let's get into the nuts and bolts of taking a powder.

1
Where to Go

The options available to the aspiring vanisher are many. Which ones you choose will be determined by many factors, including your health, savings, personal interests and preferences, and prospects for a sanctuary. Those with youth, good physical condition, and/or financial resources on their side will have a greater choice than those lacking these things, but virtually everyone can find a way to disappear by using the ideas in this chapter.

THE GREAT OUTDOORS

This is potentially the least expensive and most effective, as well as adventurous and scenic, of choices. The United States is lit-

Scenery near the Appalachian Trail.

erally covered by hiking trails, national forests, parks, wetlands, and wildlife preserves, most of which offer tremendous opportunities for solitude. You can disappear into the wilds for as long as you like, right here in the USA.

The Appalachian Trail in the East stretches over 2,000 miles from Georgia to Maine and offers clean, fresh air, fantastic views, and the chance to escape civilization almost completely. Thousands of people hike the AT (as it is known by its fans) yearly. Only a few hundred manage to finish the entire route. Most visitors are day hikers or weekend adventurers only.

Finding anonymity here is incredibly easy. An investment of a few hundred dollars in camping equipment is all you will need. Chain stores like Wal-Mart and Sports Authority, as well as local army surplus stores and flea markets, are good places to look. If you have never backpacked before, it is advisable to borrow or buy two or three books on the subject and read them thoroughly before setting out. Reasonably good physical condition is a must. So many people hike the trail every year that you can blend

**Camping supplies can be found in abundance at discount
department stores in summer and spring.**

into a sea of faces with little effort. It has all the advantages of losing yourself in the throngs of a major city, without the crime, pollution, and hostility. As long as you dress like the other hikers, remain polite but discreet in dealing with others, and behave yourself, you should have no problems.

The trail crosses roads and highways at regular intervals, and small towns are located near most entrance and exit points. Carry cash or prepaid charge cards to buy what you need, usually things like basic foods, personal items like toothpaste and soap, as well as an occasional restaurant meal. (Cards with the Mastercard or Visa logo can be purchased anonymously, with no credit references, proof of income, or even ID needed. Their value is equal to the amount you pay for them, minus a modest processing fee. The chapter on means of escape contains more information on these.) All-you-can-eat buffets are popular with hikers, and you will have no problem finding these in the communities you will pass through. All sorts of colorful-looking individuals hike part or all of the trail annually, and locals generally ignore them.

It is best to begin in early spring if you intend to go the entire distance. Most thru-hikers (the term for those who complete the entire route of 2,050 miles) start in Georgia in March or early April and trek for four to six months before reaching the other end at Mount Katahdin, Maine. A reasonably thrifty individual should be able to do the trip on $3,000 or less, including equipment.

Besides the AT, there is a sister trail along the West Coast, the Pacific Crest Trail, which is approximately as long and offers similar opportunities. There are also shorter trails located in individual states and regions of the country. For those who hate mountain climbing, the state of Florida offers hundreds of miles of trails that are virtually sidewalk-flat. Ohio is encircled by the Buckeye Trail, and in South Carolina the Palmetto Trail stretches from the mountains in the west to the beaches in the east. The Internet site www.backpacker.com is a tremendous resource for further research. Just don't buy all the hype from their advertisers and get suckered into paying too much for your equipment. A complete set of good, dependable gear can be had new for $400 or less. Check out campmor.com and majorsurplusandsurvival.com for great deals.

Not interested in doing all that walking? No problem. There are campsites galore across the nation where you can set up a tent and stay for a week or longer, up to several months. You will generally be required to show some form of ID, but there will be no background or credit checks. Private chains like KOA, as well as most larger state and national parks, offer comfortable amenities alongside the tent sites, including bathrooms with showers, washers and dryers, even vending machines, convenience stores, and restaurants. Some of these places close for the winter, but many are open year round. You can set up a large tent, a cot and sleeping bag, folding chairs and table, and relax with a good book. Cooking can be done on a camp stove (available from sporting goods stores for around $50 to $60), on a grill, or in a dutch oven suspended over your campfire. Spending time this way allows your mind and body to truly unwind, which is important when you are trying to gather your thoughts and evaluate your options. Keep your site clean, stay reasonably quiet, and behave yourself, and you should have no problems.

A good tent is essential to camping comfort.
Here the author poses proudly after erecting his.

There is one other outdoors option which provides ultimate anonymity, and that is hiding out in the woods, deep in the forest or other wilderness where humans never go. This is an option for those who do not wish to be seen by others, and it offers complete privacy if done right. The thing to remember is that the United States is filled with remote places that people never trod. Most of the Great Smoky Mountains National Park, for example, is totally uninhabited. Its holdings include more than 10 million acres of pristine wild lands. Avoid the public campsites, established trails, and scenic roads, and you can remain undiscovered forever.

Accused antiabortion terrorist and Olympic bomber Eric Rudolph lived for five years in the Smoky Mountains without being seen, despite a massive effort on the part of law enforcement and professional bounty hunters to find him. Eventually he was spotted by a local cop in Murphy, North Carolina, and arrested. Had he not wandered into town to raid Dumpsters, he would probably still be free.

They say Bigfoot lives in the Rocky Mountains out West. If so, then he has done an excellent job hiding, because he has been hunted by countless thousands and never captured. I have seen the Olympic National Forest in western Washington State, as well as the mountainous parts of Wyoming, Montana, and Idaho. It would be no problem getting lost in those areas. The southwest is largely desert, but it is dotted by abandoned ghost towns that tourists do not frequent. Desert survival is an art unto itself but has been accomplished for long periods of time.

Living this way would have its share of risks as well as advantages. You are on your own if you break a leg or need emergency surgery to remove your appendix. There is much to consider if you choose this option. Fortunately, companies like Paladin Press (www.paladin-press.com) and Loompanics (www.loompanics.com) sell outstanding books on wilderness survival, and I refer you to their catalogs. For those who love the outdoors and can face its challenges, living on a hiking trail, in a campground, or just out in the middle of nowhere can offer sanctuary as well as adventure.

Remember Unlucky in Love Larry? This is the option he took. He spent the night at a rest stop, stopped at a branch of his bank first thing the next morning, and emptied out the checking and savings accounts. He also maxed out his credit cards (and then cancelled them), using them to get cash advances and buy supplies. Fortunately, he had done enough research on the AT to realize what kind of equipment he would need, so a couple of trips to sporting goods stores were all that it took to outfit him. Now he is staying at a mountain cabin for a couple of weeks, doing all the day hiking and exercising he can to prepare for the big walk ahead. Yes, he sweats a lot, but he never hears his wife's nagging voice. That has to be nice . . .

THE OPEN ROAD

This option is closely related to the last one, in that you will be spending a great deal of time outside. However, instead of being out in the woods or the desert, you are on the highway with your thumb out. Hitchhiking is a great low-cost way to see the country. Despite its seedy reputation, it is much safer and more pleasant than most people think.

You will carry your possessions in a duffel bag or backpack. You are likely to meet nearly anyone when you hitchhike, but most people who give you rides will fall into three different categories:

1) Born-again Christians who want you to accept Jesus.
2) Old men who want you to listen to their stories of the old days.
3) Homosexuals who want your ass. Generally, the first two types are more abundant, unless you are hitching a ride anywhere near San Francisco. Horror stories in the media aside, it is rare that hitchers are assaulted or killed. (Special note to women: Forget this option. Don't argue with me; just forget it. We both know why.)

The whole adventure of hitchhiking is in the uncertainty. You never know from day to day whom you will meet, what you will eat, or where you will sleep. I have hitched a little myself, but my ex-hippy brother is an old master of the art. He has thumbed his way from Atlanta to the West Coast more than once. He advises the following:

1) Dress in casual, durable clothes that are neat and clean—i.e., jeans and a T-shirt, with a heavy shirt and/or jacket in winter and a hat of some kind to protect your head from the sun and the wind. Wear nothing that makes you look as if you might be rich (e.g., nice jewelry, fine watch; you get the idea). Duffel bags and backpacks are good for carrying your stuff. Make sure they look old.
2) Use of a cardboard sign with the name of your destination on it can be helpful. Make sure the letters are big and easily read.
3) Be courteous to the people who pick you up, but feel free to decline a ride with anyone who creeps you out.
4) Take a tarp with you to protect you from the rain and snow. A tarp can be wrapped up in like a sleeping bag or made into an impromptu tent. Also, a military-style sleeping bag and

light pup tent can spare you from endless discomfort. Buy them cheap and stuff them in your bag or pack.

5) Sleeping is best done under bridges, he claims. I have also heard that church graveyards are comfortable spots. On very cold evenings, he would crawl under a bridge and wrap himself up in plastic.

6) Don't hassle the cops and they usually won't hassle you. Kiss their ass if necessary, but never, ever challenge a cop's authority.

My brother also shared some fascinating stories with me, which should give you a good idea of what you may expect. One of these involved an evening in Houston, during which he saw a man die in the middle of the street from a slit throat. This motivated him and his traveling companions to seek shelter for the night, and, by pooling their financial resources, they were able to rent a motel room. Unbeknownst to them, the flop was actually a cover for a cat house, which they discovered when they went upstairs and found the hallway lined with women in various states of undress loudly proclaiming their services.

Having no money to pay for such services, my brother and his three male companions went to their room. This caused the ladies to conclude that they were gay. The gentleman in charge of the house, himself a flaming homosexual, was delighted to hear this, and my brother and his friends spent much of the night declining his advances.

Things were especially hard for one friend who ventured to the rest room at the end of the hall to shower. He panicked when the manager decided he would shower with him.

His other tales from the road ranged from fleeing mentally disturbed drivers to suffering from hypothermia to smoking cigarettes infested with weevils. But he also had stories of seeing beautiful areas of the country, meeting kind and interesting people, and enjoying a sense of freedom he has never known since.

Good luck out there if you decide to hitchhike. For further research, consult *The Hitchhiker's Handbook* from Loompanics.

The author is dressed for hitchhiking success. Note simple but durable clothes. Personal items are in old bag he carries.

For the nonsuperstitious, cemeteries make comfortable, safe places to sleep.

THE STREET

While not the most pleasant choice in this chapter, living as a homeless person may be an option for those who have little money and/or desire almost complete anonymity. Street people are a common sight in most decent-sized cities these days, not just metropolises like Atlanta and New York. You will probably never be noticed among the masses of people who sleep in the alleys, rescue missions, or doorways.

Athens, Georgia, is a good example of a smaller city (population approximately 100,000 to 200,000) where the homeless are well tolerated. There is an abundance of benches in the downtown area where the transient population gathers to socialize and to feed off whatever they are given or can find. Athens is a university town, so there are plenty of guilt-ridden white liberals and young, out-of-touch idealists to sponge off of. The abundance of restaurants and coffeehouses means edible food is just a Dumpster dive away. Being a Southern city,

Athens enjoys a mild to moderate climate year 'round, though the summers can be quite hot.

Athens has a very visible downtown police presence, but the cops generally do not hassle the homeless as long as they are well-behaved. Free or low-cost entertainment can be had from the countless small bands that play the clubs up and down Clayton Avenue. Street musicians are common as well. There is always an outdoor play, political demonstration, or something else going on. Reading material is abundant; 'zines can be purchased very cheaply from Bizarro Wuxtry's, the local comic book shop. (My favorite is "Betty and Judy," an illustrated 'zine about two adolescent girls who annoy old men and beat up obnoxious convenience store clerks. It runs 10 cents a copy.) I have taken clean and virtually unread newspapers from the trashcans when I didn't want to spend the 50 cents for my own copy. The University of Georgia library is very accessible. It has literally millions of books, papers, and other publications. My brother goes into the magazine shops downtown and reads articles at the stand, then puts them back on the shelf without purchasing anything. He has never been hassled for this.

All in all, Athens would be one of the better places to be homeless for a while if circumstances ever made it necessary. I urge you to strongly consider using a college or university town for your sanctuary, no matter which of the options in this chapter you decide to use. The casual, transitory atmosphere is perfect for someone trying not to be noticed.

You will need a good sleeping bag, plastic sheet or tarp for protection from the rain, and a backpack or duffel bag to hold your possessions. I advise against carrying a firearm; it can backfire on you in many ways (pun intended). A large can of pepper spray or handheld stun gun might be okay. The best weapon you can have is your wits. Always be aware of what is happening around you.

Living on the street is another option that requires long and hard thought. Done right, in the proper location, it can be tolerable. For those seriously contemplating it, I highly recommend the book *Surviving on the Street: How to Go Down without*

Going Out by Ace Backwords (available from Paladin Press). It is absolutely the best book on homelessness I have ever seen. Ace lived on the mean streets of San Francisco for years, so his advice is all real-world, not academic BS. *Dumpster Diving: The Advanced Course* is another outstanding resource offered by Paladin Press. Put your prejudices aside; Dumpsters are veritable treasure troves filled with all sorts of goodies in great condition. Fresh food, clothing, building materials, even items suitable for resale are thrown away in abundance every day, and you can get them for *free*. Learn to live off of the wastefulness of American society, and you will always live well.

HOTELS/MOTELS/BOARDING HOUSES/TRAILER PARKS

For the less adventurous, renting a place can prove to be a viable alternative to the above-described options. Hotels and boarding houses offer two advantages to conventional rentals: one does not normally have to submit to background or credit checks, and electricity, water, and local phone service are generally included in the rent. In addition, many trailer parks offer renters a package deal that includes the cost of electricity and water. This circumvents the need to establish these utilities in one's own name.

This said, there are disadvantages to these options as well. The most troublesome of these is that your future neighbors may not be the sort of people you want to be around. Rent-by-the-week motels have an especially bad reputation. Drug dealers and prostitutes often live out of them. When I resided in Georgia there were a pair of inns just outside of town that were always getting raided by the sheriff's department. There was a man who worked for me for a while who lived in one of them. He told me he did not dare to go outside his room after dark. The potential for trouble was too great.

Traveling work crews often stay in these kinds of hotels. They can range from tired construction workers just wanting a good night's sleep to real rowdies looking for drinking, drugs, and a fight. Ladies of the evening prowl the parking lot or even knock

Extended-stay hotels like this one are clean, quiet, and safe.

on one door after another, seeking customers. Ditto for the dope dealers. For a long time conditions like these were the norm for those who sought weekly or monthly lodging in motels. In the last several years this has begun to change. Clean, decent chains have sprung up across the country. They cater to business travelers and others who may need to reside away from home for a while. They often have the words "extended stay" in their names. I lived in one of these in Pennsylvania for a while and found it a wonderful place. The room was set up like a small apartment with a kitchenette, desk, and recliner. There was a fitness room and snack bar on the premises, and private boxes were available for the guests to receive mail. If you choose to stay in a motel during your absence, I strongly recommend seeking out a place like this. Rates are generally $150 to $200 per week, and they take cash. A driver's license, which is in no way verified as authentic, is usually sufficient identification to check in. I discuss alternate ID later in the book. (I am assuming, of course, that you are the kind of person who likes things calm and peaceful. On the other hand, you may be the sort who enjoys the company of flesh peddlers, drug dealers, and violent people. If so, save your bucks and go for the cheap dives you can live in for a hundred bucks a week. Just don't be surprised if you end up on *COPS* one night for all the world to gawk at.)

Boarding houses used to be very common but are hard to find these days. There was one in Belton, South Carolina, that I stayed in for a couple of months. The manager was a convicted felon who wore an alarm around his ankle that would go off if he left the property. He was under house arrest for receiving stolen goods. There was a very homely, mannish-looking slut across the hall who always wanted sex from me (no, I didn't accommodate her). Various kinds of losers rented the other bedrooms. The house was a giant two-story affair that used to be a funeral parlor. We shared a common bathroom and had a telephone downstairs with local service.

The "manager" would get plastered at night and scream at his wife. He eventually went back to prison for beating her half to death one night. Sometimes he would corner me downstairs and regale me with tales of his "glorious" criminal past. I found his stories difficult to believe.

I moved as soon as I could and rented a bedroom in a private home. My landlady was semiretired and took in boarders to supplement her income. She cooked dinner for her tenants at night, and we would all watch TV in her big living room in the evening. This was a really decent arrangement and accommodated me for several months.

The lesson here is to check out any motel, boarding house, or trailer park carefully. There are still decent places among them. Chosen carefully, these can be excellent options for those who have the cash. Keep your nose clean, be polite but discreet when talking to others, and feel free to lie as much as necessary about your real situation, both on the rental application as well as person-to-person. In rare cases you may need to provide real references to rent in a boarding house or trailer park. (By "real" I mean the landlord or lady will actually try to verify them. I discuss establishing false references in a later chapter.)

RENTAL HOUSE OR APARTMENT

This option presents limited opportunities for the disappearee, but there are some drawbacks. Houses and apartments generally require a fair degree of paperwork as well as a good supply of cash. Credit and background checks are common. In addition, it is usually necessary for tenants to provide their own utilities, which means signing up with the local electric company and the city water service. The vanisher can use a fraudulent Social Security number to do so, but this can be risky and will almost always necessitate a hefty deposit, unless he or she has already obtained credit under the number. It is unlikely that anyone should go to such measures merely to stage a short-term disappearance.

Houses and apartments need to be furnished, although they often come with a stove and refrigerator in place. In addition, at least in the case of houses, you will likely be surrounded by people who have lived in the community for a while. They will see you as their new neighbor and may try to get to know you; this could be very bad for someone maintaining a low profile. The local authorities may check you out, just to make sure a "trouble-maker" is not invading their peaceful little town. If you have brought your car, your out-of-town or out-of-state plates will draw attention. All in all, this option should be avoided if possible.

An exception may be if you have a close relative or friend who owns a rental home, timeshare, or summer/vacation dwelling and is willing to let you use it. Sometimes members of religious or political groups have networks of fellow adherents that will assist them. That leads directly into the next option.

SHELTER OR SAFE HOUSE

Abused women can take refuge in any one of hundreds of shelters set up for them. Many of these will shelter their children as well. There are tons of resources available for women in this situation, and I list some of them in Appendix I at the back of this book. Check out carefully any place you consider, and make sure they can take you in for as long as you need to be away from home.

If you are a member of a political, racial, or religious group that is frequently persecuted, then there may already be a network of safe houses around the country ready to assist you. Check with others of your color or creed on this option. Also refer to the suggestions for further reading at the back of this book.

In my research on this option, I discovered that there are essentially three different types of women's shelters across the country. One of these is the government-funded variety, often known as the "county shelter." The advantage of these is that they are adequately if not generously funded, enjoy strong support from local law enforcement, and are free or very low cost to the women who use them. The primary disadvantage is that bed space may be severely limited and so women may only be able to stay there for a few days. Check with your city or county's social services agencies to see if they support such a shelter and what kind of services it offers.

An alternative to the county shelter is one run by a private organization that is nonreligious. These are often feminist groups with local chapters. The conditions at these places vary widely. Some are clean, decent places for battered women and their children to live temporarily while they straighten their lives out. Others are little more than holding cells that treat the women like cattle. Some have been investigated numerous times for mistreatment and misuse of funds. For example, several shelters in the United States and Canada have come under criticism for refusing to allow the women to have male visitors, even if the person in question was their attorney, minister, or physician!

Homes like this are often run by ultrafeminists who equate anyone who does not have to sit down to urinate with Satan himself. I advise that you do research on any home in which you are considering seeking shelter. Check with law enforcement, civic groups, and other charities in the area to find out what kind of a reputation the place has.

The final alternative is a shelter run by a church or other religious group. These are subject to the same uncertainties I have already outlined, with the additional proviso that they will see you as a target for evangelistic work if you do not agree with their beliefs. If you are a nonreligious person with no interest in acquiring a faith, you may find this to be more than you can take. Then again, when you are flat broke, cold, and hungry, what is so bad about hearing a sermon if you know there is soup and a warm bed waiting afterward? Check these homes out the same way you would the other options. Even if you cannot stay at one of these places for very long, you can usually get shelter for at least a few days while you flesh out other options.

Remember Sally from the last chapter? She was able to obtain shelter at a church-affiliated home for battered women. The situation is not ideal; she does not really want to receive Jesus as her savior, but the staff is pretty insistent about it. Still, they are not beating her or letting her or the baby starve, so it is a definite improvement over her last situation. We will check in on her again later.

SECRET HIDING PLACE

If there is an abandoned home, a shack in the woods, or a hidden cellar that only you know about, then you have a refuge ready to go. Stock your sanctuary with canned foods or MREs, first aid supplies, and anything else you may need for a while. The book *The Modern Survival Retreat* from Paladin Press is a great resource for further study.

A PRIVATE HOME

If you have a "covert" friend somewhere, he or she may be willing to put you up for a while. The Internet can be a great place to meet people like you who are open to new people and new experiences. It can also be a wonderful place to meet people who will slit your throat and toss your carcass in the river. Be careful.

Relatives may put you up, but any pursuers will logically think you are staying with family and probably seek them out. When I was a teenager, I went to stay with my aunt after my father came home in a drunken rage one night and tried to shoot me. She did not live far from him, but he did not dare bother me at her house. My aunt was heavily armed and a great shot.

There is one more option I want to mention here, which can be helpful to those in need of ending their marriage. The state of Nevada is a great place to get a quickie divorce, and you only have to "live" there for six weeks before you are officially a resident.

2
Unloading

Made up your mind which option is best for you? Then let's turn the page and start getting ready for the great escape.

Okay, you have searched your soul, evaluated your options, and decided to get the hell out of Dodge for a while. Now it is time to prepare for the big escape. And if you're really going to take off, you've got to lighten your load.

WHAT TO DO WITH YOUR STUFF

Unless you are an extreme minimalist, it is unlikely that you will be able to take all of your crap with you. In most cases you would not want to anyway. The less you have to fuss with material possessions, the more you will be able to think about your situation. So travel light. Take basic clothes, personal care/hygiene items, a few essential books, and maybe some music CDs or cassettes and a handheld player, and try to leave behind as much as possible. There are three things you can do with the stuff you don't take with you and don't want to throw away.

Store It
The storage option usually entails renting a storage building by the month and stashing your gear there for the time you will be gone. There are operations all over the country that lease sheds for this purpose. You will usually pay the first month's rent plus a small deposit and sign an agreement that says the owner can confiscate your goods if you fall behind on the payments. Most of the time you will have to be behind three months or more before he can exercise this option. Don't tell the manager about your plans to take a powder, however. This will probably spook him or her. Simply pack the stuff in, secure the big metal door with your own padlock, and that is it.

Since you supply the padlock, the owner or manager does not have a key and thus cannot poke around your belongings. Theft is unlikely, since these facilities are surrounded by high fences with gates that are locked at night.

You have to visit your unit during operating hours, or, at an additional cost, you can often get a private access code that will disarm the security system and allow you to enter at any time. My brother used to visit his in the middle of the night. He met hookers sometimes hanging around outside the facility. He reports that they were more trouble than they were worth.

This is an excellent option most of the time (storing, not meeting hookers), but there are a few things to consider. First, these storage facilities vary widely in cost, service, and quality. In the South it is easy to rent a unit for $50 or less a month that should hold an entire house full of belongings—for example, a 10' x 10' space with a very high ceiling to allow stuff to be stacked up. The same space in some Yankee states could easily

Storage facilities vary in quality. This one offers security and good rates.

A fence surrounding the units adds to security.

set you back $200 a month or more! (I don't know why this is; probably some ridiculous Big-Brother-type laws. The northeastern states are run like socialist dictatorships.) Check the rates to make sure you can swing the payments for the duration of your absence.

You want to make sure the shed is reasonably weatherproof. I rented a unit in South Carolina with a leaky roof, and my junk got soaked with the first rain. Generally, the more permanent the outfit looks the better it is. A quality operation will have sheds that are lined with brick and have shingle roofs. There will be a substantial metal fence surrounding the location, and plenty of night lighting. These facilities may cost a few dollars more per month than the ones that look like an abandoned chicken farm, but they are worth it.

You will want to get some tarps to cover your stuff with, and, while you are at it, put some rat and mouse bait on the floor to keep vermin from nesting in your books and clothing. Seal everything snugly in heavy cardboard boxes, or, even better, plastic or metal bins or barrels. Remember that there is no climate control normally; your stuff will fry in summer and freeze in winter. This matters little unless you are storing perishable goods. If you have items that are heat- or cold-sensitive, there are storage facilities that offer temperature control for their units. They are not cheap.

Remember Working Man Jack? He had a very difficult decision to make about his truck, and finally he concluded that putting it in a storage building was the best option for him. Repo men (and I say this as someone who used to do skip tracing as well as assign and work closely with repossession agents) are relentless and ruthless. Since Jack would be staying with a relative in his state, he could never be sure they had not found him. Even if his brother had fenced-in property and a big dog, the truck would still be vulnerable at Jack's work site, as well as anywhere he drove it.

Repo men have shadowed people for miles, snatching their targeted cars when the owners went into the grocery or convenience store. They have pretended to be law enforcement agents with arrest warrants, paid off neighbors to snitch on people whose vehicles they were after, and done plenty of other nasty things. They do not have souls.

Unless you are relocating to a place far, far away (preferably in another state), and unless you have been extremely careful not to establish a paper trail or even tell anyone where you are going, then they will find you. By the way, Jack rented the storage building using fake ID, a subject we will cover later. He obtained the unit in a town he had never been in before, a good distance from his old haunts as well as where his brother lives. He sends his payments through a mail drop, and he is *very* careful to make sure they are received on time. In addition, he moved the truck into the storage building late at night when no one was around. It is extremely unlikely that any repossession agent will find it.

There are special concerns to be aware of if you plan to store firearms, ammunition, medicine, or foodstuffs. If this is your situation, I suggest you consult one of the many excellent publications available from Paladin Press or Loompanics on caching sensitive items. The longer you are away, the more important proper storage techniques become. *How to Bury Your Goods: The Complete Manual of Long Term Underground Storage* from Loompanics is an excellent resource on this topic.

Don't want to store your stuff? Then the next option is to . . .

Sell It

I recommend this avenue highly, for several different reasons. First off, most people have way too much useless junk— things they will never need and rarely if ever use. To prove this to yourself, do a little exercise. Walk around your house and see how much stuff you have that you have not used in several months or years. Don't forget the basement, attic, or garage, or that "spare" bedroom that is too cluttered to sleep in.

Holding onto all this junk is bad for many reasons. First off, it clutters the mind. There is a reason that hermits, sages, and wise men have practiced asceticism throughout the ages. Excessive possessions prohibit clarity of thought, and the one thing you need right now is a clear head. Secondly, those items can be turned into cash, which is always useful. As an example, a couple of years back I went through the small trailer I was living in and boxed up all the stuff I had bought and never used. I carried it down to the local flea market, where it covered two big tables and a little more, and sold it for whatever price folks would offer to pay. By the end of the weekend I made more than $500. You can do the same. Thirdly, limiting one's possessions is a good discipline. Americans spend too much, charge too much, and save far too little. Learning to live with less is a good way to clear up money to invest, a habit that is essential to a secure future.

Think about it for a moment: are the problems that you are trying to get away from at least partially tied to financial concerns? In most cases, I'll bet they are. Your disappearance may be a good time to assess your life and figure out what is really important. The point is this: you should try to learn how to use money, instead of allowing money to use you. For further research on this topic, I highly recommend the book *The Richest Man in Babylon*, available at virtually any bookstore. It is a short but highly illuminating read.

A yard or garage sale is a good way to dispose of unwanted items. Like any worthwhile endeavor, it requires a little planning. Visit some sales in your area if you have never held one of your own, so you can see how it is done. You want to be careful to price things appropriately. Since you are raising funds to finance your disappearance, you probably want to set them fairly low in order to boost sales.

Place an ad in the local paper, put signs up around the neighborhood a few days in advance announcing the event, and be prepared to get up early on the day of the sale. Many people who frequent these are early birds hoping to get the proverbial worm. Saturday mornings are by far the best time to sell. If you can, it is a good idea to set the stuff outside on tables the night before and cover the merchandise with tarps that you clamp or weigh down.

Use tags to display the prices clearly. Some people pass on buying things because they are too shy to ask how much they are. Use tables to display the merchandise if possible; if not, lay a tarp, blankets, or a sheet on the driveway or on the ground, and place the items on top. Be sure to have plenty of coins and small bills to make change with. Taking checks is always a risk; I advise against it unless you know and trust the person well.

Sally had a very successful yard sale right before she left for the shelter. She made well over $1,000, disposing not only of her own unwanted items but also her abusive boyfriend's bass boat, which he had left parked on a trailer in her backyard. Silly man.

An alternative to a yard or garage sale is the local flea market. Look in the Yellow Pages for the nearest one, or just ask around if you don't already know where the closest one is. Be sure to check the weather forecast for the day you plan to sell. Nothing kills a good flea market day like rain. Most markets have tables that are outside, as well as some that are under shelters or indoors.

The market owner makes his money by charging the dealers rent for the tables. This is usually a very reasonable fee, as low as $3 for an outside spot. You can prepay your rent at the market office before sale day, or just show up early in the morning, set up your wares, and wait for the manager to come by and collect it personally. Try to display your stuff clearly and neatly, and set as much on each table as you can to save on rental expenses. As with the yard sale, showing up early is important. Some markets are already crowded by 6 A.M. on a weekend day!

Your setup need not look like a display counter at Saxs Fifth Avenue, but it should be clean, neat, and attractive. Clean and dust any wares that need it. Glass cleaner works great on paperback book covers. Books by well-known authors are usually good sellers, by the way. Make sure you are clean and neat as well. Jeans and a T-shirt are just fine. You should wear some sort of hat to protect your head from the sun. Sunscreen and/or a beach umbrella can come in handy on hot spring or summer days. You will need a chair to sit in behind your tables. Bring plenty of coins and small bills for change, just as with the yard sale. Pack a lunch and plenty to drink.

Pricing can be tricky. The best guide is what other dealers are charging for similar items. Try to undercut them if you can. Don't worry about their feelings; this is business. Sometimes another dealer will come by and offer to buy most or all of your stuff for a lump sum. This is usually not a good idea unless it is near the end of the sale day. Hagglers will sometimes try to get you to come down on the price you have set. If it is an item that others have looked at or asked about, then it is best to stand firm.

A pickup truck or van is usually the best vehicle to haul your stuff in, but any vehicle will do. For years I carried my merchandise to market in a Ford Escort crammed with boxes full of items. A 4' x 8' or similarly sized utility trailer can be useful to load your wares on. These can be pulled by the smallest of cars easily.

If it sounds like I have experience selling at flea markets and yard sales, it is because I do. They are great ways of earning extra cash. The most important "secret" to the business is what kind of merchandise to sell. Way too many novice dealers make the mistake of buying so-called "quick sell" items from wholesalers, such as T-shirts, sunglasses, watches, porcelain figurines and off-brand tools. When they get to market, they see row after row of competing dealers selling virtually the same items. Nobody makes any money this way.

Auctions are far better sources for good, salable products. My favorites are the ones held periodically by storage building sites. When a tenant does not pay the rent on a unit for several months, which happens all the time, then the owner can exercise his right to confiscate the stored items and sell them off to recoup his losses. The auction is announced in the local paper, or you can call the office to find out when the next one will be. Often you can buy a shed full of furniture, books, clothes, tools, entertainment electronics, and other goodies for a couple hundred dollars or less. The profit margin can be considerable when you resell, even if you charge low prices. For those interested in pursuing this subject, I recommend the book *How To Make Cash Money Selling at Swap Meets, Flea Markets, Etc.* by Jordan L. Cooper, published by Loompanics.

Ooops, almost forgot—you may want to consider selling your stuff by using the classifieds section of your local paper, if you don't mind advertising your intentions to get rid of the stuff. Check with the editor or look online for information on rates and so on.

If you don't want or need to sell or store your stuff, the final option is the simplest . . .

Flea markets are great places to buy or sell goods.

Storage building auctions can be great sources of salable merchandise.

Give It Away

This option is simple, charitable, and often tax-deductible. Despite wearisome rantings about "cold-hearted, selfish Americans" by loser liberal types, ours is a generous and compassionate land. Virtually every community has a church or social agency that accepts donations of goods. These are either given or sold at very low cost to the poor.

The Salvation Army and Goodwill Industries operate thrift stores nationwide that are eager to receive your unwanted stuff. You can get a receipt for your donations that will reduce your tax bill in April; consult your attorney or accountant for specific information. Even automobiles are taken for charitable purposes, and the tax write-off for giving one away can be significant.

One word of caution: I would avoid telling any of the charity workers you come in contact with about your plans for escaping for a while, unless you know they can refer you to a shelter or safe house that will help you. Anyone you share your plans with is a potential snitch. Keep your own counsel as much as possible. And bless you for giving to the disadvantaged.

Oh, yeah! If all else fails, you can always abandon your stuff and let someone else worry about it. Neither neat nor pretty, this option is one of last resort. Unlucky in Love Larry did it. Now his wayward wife has to figure out how to make the payments. Maybe she had better start charging for her services. . . .

Now that you've unloaded all of the stuff you don't need, let's look at something you will need: money.

3

Financial Concerns

The more cash you have the better off you will be, no matter which route you choose to disappear. Even hitchhikers and campers need money for food and personal items. Those using more conventional means to escape will need money for hotel rooms, gas, and so on.

Plain old greenbacks are usually preferable to checks or credit cards. Personal checks leave a paper trail and are increasingly viewed with distrust. Credit cards leave a paper trail as well; also, if you are fleeing an abusive or unfaithful spouse whose name is on the account, he or she can easily cancel the card. My advice is to get cash advances on your cards and then forget them.

There is a scenario in which using credit or debit cards may prove to your advantage in misleading potential pursuers. I call this strategy the "going from Atlanta to New York by way of Seattle route." Let's say you are fleeing Dixie for the Big Apple. Instead of a straight path, you go the scenic route, driving well out of your way to the west, say, to Seattle. On the way you make liberal use of your credit cards, establishing a clear trail for investigators to follow to the West Coast. Upon arriving in Seattle, you apply for a checking and savings account at a local bank using a bogus address. You may also fill out a rent application with any apartment complex or other rental property. You then ditch the card and drive to your real destination back east, using only cash to pay for purchases.

If you are using public transportation, you can establish a paper trail in a similar fashion by making purchases along the way at bus or train stops, or, if traveling by air, by charging items in the airport shops. The idea is to create a paper trail that leads any investigators in a completely wrong direction. While they are trying to find you in a city thousands of miles away from where you are, you kick back and laugh your ass off.

The one drawback to using cash is the possibility of being robbed or just losing it. Many people like to use traveler's checks, which are guaranteed against loss or theft.

This is generally safe, but some new-identity experts caution that it can create a paper trail. To minimize this possibility, I advise buying the checks at several different financial institutions as far apart as possible, buying as small a quantity as possible at each one. You will need to show identification to buy traveler's checks. (I did not say it had to be legitimate ID.)

Another alternative is using money orders. Many merchants are hesitant about accepting these. I suggest purchasing U.S. Postal Service money orders for amounts of $100 or less. As with the traveler's checks, buy from as many different post offices as possible. Any local post office in the country will cash one of these. Make it out to yourself, and, again, be prepared to show some ID. If this concerns you, then read the section on false identification coming up later.

Since money can often buy them, the next subjects we should logically consider are friends, family, and confederates.

KEEPING IN TOUCH

People can be your greatest assets or your biggest headaches, depending on a number of factors. A supportive and trustworthy person or persons can be of enormous help to you during the planning phase as well as the actual disappearance. On the other hand, they are potential security risks, especially if they know where you can be found. You must weigh the advantages against the risks when determining whether to let anyone know what you have planned.

When I took a powder, the only person I informed was my older, ex-hippy brother, who was totally cool about the whole thing. He kept my secret and told snoops who called him that I was missing and presumed dead in New York City. This discouraged their investigative efforts greatly. Of course, he knew I was alive and well and not anywhere near New York (or was I?).

Before deciding to tell anyone your plans, you need to do some hard thinking. Can you endure being away from people you care about and knowing they are probably worried about you? You have to weigh your desire to keep in touch with family or friends against the possibility that everyone will find out your plans.

Are there any scenarios you can imagine (within reason) where you will need to contact an acquaintance? Maybe there is a sick relative whose situation is tenuous, and you want to keep updated on this person. Perhaps you are leaving children in someone else's care while you hide from a spouse who has threatened to kill you. You will want to know that they are okay. There may be legal or financial affairs you need to keep abreast of. This information could be critical to knowing when it is safe to resurface.

For many people, separating themselves from family and friends may be traumatic, especially if they know their disappearance may last several months or more. Others are glad to say good riddance to "those bastards." This is a choice you must make for yourself. In general, it is best to tell no one, unless you feel you can trust the person completely.

Sally and Unlucky Larry chose to remain completely undercover. It was especially hard on Sally, but the counselors at the shelter persuaded her that it was for the best. They were right. Jack still kept discreet contact with old friends but told no one where his truck was. No one.

There is a way to maintain contact with acquaintances that is very secure and will allow you to protect your privacy. That is by using a mail drop.

Sending and Receiving Mail

There is virtually nothing more useful to seekers of privacy than a mail forwarding service, known commonly as a "mail drop." These have proliferated in recent years, and virtually every community in the United States has one in town or nearby (including the giant metropolis of Moonville, South Carolina). Mailboxes Etc. is the most common one, with more than 3,000 locations from coast to coast.

Following are some of the advantages mail drops offer:

- They will allow you to receive mail without anyone knowing your location. You can even throw people off the trail with mail drops, causing them to think you are somewhere other than where you really are.
- You can deal with creditors while keeping them at bay. This can be invaluable to those who are trying to pay off a vehicle or other mortgaged item and are afraid the repo man will come after them if the bank finds out where they are. (Working Man Jack used mail drops to send payments to his finance company without their discovering where he was.)
- Mail drops usually offer numerous services besides mail forwarding, including private mailbox rental. They often ship and receive packages for UPS and Federal Express. They also offer money orders, low-cost photocopying, stationary and office supplies, desktop publishing, and 24-hour access to your mailbox.

Mail drops offer the best way to stay in touch with selected individuals while keeping your real location a secret. This is how it is done: before you take off, go to a local service and rent a mailbox. The cost will generally run from $8 to $12 a month. You can usually rent the box for up to a year at a time or as little as 90 days.

Advise the owner or manager that you will be out of town for a while and will need mail forwarded to you. Make up some bland, believable story, such as the company is transferring you or you have to care for a sick friend or relative for a while. Provide the new address where you will be during your disappearance, if you have it yet. If not, advise the manager that you will call or mail him or her soon with your temporary new address. Mail Drops will charge a fee for forwarding the mail to you, but this is usually quite reasonable.

For best security, I highly recommend renting another box at a mail drop near the place where you will be seeking refuge and giving this address to the first place as your forwarding address. Mail drop employees are generally very good at guarding their customers' privacy (and in fact can be sued if they divulge information about their clients to anyone other than law enforcement agents with the proper authorizations), but there have been situations in which some have been bribed or otherwise coerced into revealing a person's whereabouts. If you cannot find a private mail drop near your refuge, then a P.O. box rented from the local post office should suffice. A word of caution: do not use a regular P.O. box in the local post office if you can rent one from a private service instead. Private detectives and seasoned investigators have several tricks for getting forwarding addresses and other supposedly confidential data from postal employees. The official U.S. Postal Service (USPS) Web site (www.usps.com/cpim/ftp/pubs/pub549/pub549.htm) states that individuals serving legal process papers may obtain forwarding addresses. Imagine a maniacal spouse filing for divorce, using this as an excuse to obtain his soon-to-be-ex's current address in order to serve notice on her. When he does discover her whereabouts, he dissolves the union with a .44 Magnum instead of a court decree. Don't let this happen to you.

Besides receiving mail, you may need or want to send letters to people in your old world from time to time. If you simply mail them from the area you are taking refuge in, then you run the risk of compromising your privacy. Even if you do not put a return address on the envelope, the recipient, as well as anyone else who sees the envelope, will view the postmark and know your general location. There are two possible solutions to this:

- Travel away from your refuge occasionally to send mail. The further you can get away the better.
- Use a remailing service. This is a business that will receive mail from you and then remail it from its location. This allows the recipient to see the service's postmark only, not yours. The mail drop that you set up in the place you left may provide this service. If not, there are an abundance of companies that do this around the country. It pays to be careful when choosing one; consult the Better Business Bureau in the area to find one that is established and reliable. I list resources in the back of the book that you can use to find out more about mail drops and remailing services.

In the case of Sally, the people who run her shelter have a system in place for her to communicate with family without giving away her location. Shelters tend to be very good at this sort of thing. Unlucky Larry has no desire to keep in touch with anyone from his old world, so he does not use the mail.

There are a couple of precautions I would advise taking when using mail drops. First, avoid accepting any certified or registered mail. These can be used by investigators trying to verify your current whereabouts. Second, try to check your mail at odd hours and different times each day. Finally, be wary of accepting any large, strangely shaped, or oddly colored packages that you are not expecting. If someone is shadowing the location and sees you walking out with the item, then your cover is blown. Third, beware of any correspondence you receive offering you a prize, advising you of a coming "reunion" of any sort, or urging you to respond to it. These are all methods used to find people who are using mail drops for privacy. I don't mean to make you unnecessarily paranoid with all this talk. (I myself hate being paranoid, but I have no choice, with so many people against me.)

Mail drops and remailing services have endless uses, and the subject is broader than what I can cover here. If you wish to know more, I recommend the book How To Use Mail Drops for Profit, Privacy, and Self-Protection, available from Loompanics. A directory of mail drops is The Worldwide Maildrop Guide, published by Eden Press (www.edenpress.com).

There are other ways of keeping in touch besides physical mail. The best and cheapest of these is e-mail. You can set up a free electronic mail address from services like Hotmail (www.hotmail.com) that will let you check your messages from any computer that has Internet access. You will be asked to provide personal information in exchange for the free service. Lie.

You do not want to transfer or set up an Internet account in your new location; this can create a trail right to you. You may be staying with people who already have an account and will let you use theirs. If not, the local public library may have public access computers you can use.

There are now companies that offer prepaid Internet service. You buy a CD-Rom at a local computer, office, or convenience store and receive a limited amount of time on the 'Net. The last time I checked, 10 hours of Web time could be purchased prepaid for about 10 bucks. You sign no credit agreements, the prepaid service can be accessed from virtually anywhere, and you give no personal information to the vendor, so you can use it with anonymity.

Phone calls to your old world are usually not a good idea unless made some distance from your normal location. If you do need to keep in touch with a confederate, prepaid phone cards are available from major retailers and convenience stores. A prepaid cellular phone is a way of having wireless phone service without applying for credit. Which brings us to the subject of credit.

CREDIT

It is time we discussed that all-important subject. I strongly recommend against using credit for any reason while you are taking a powder. If you "put it on the card" once while in your area of refuge, you have blown it. You might as well get a bullhorn and ride through town shouting, "Hey everybody, here I am!" Your pursuers will find you if they are even halfway trying. This is especially true if you brought a financed vehicle or other mortgaged item with you, or if you left your creditors in the lurch when you took off.

If you absolutely must make purchases that require using a credit or debit card, then your only real option is to find someone who will let you use theirs. They will actually make the purchase in their name, and you pay them for it in cash in exchange for the merchandise when it arrives. Needless to say, there must be a strong bond of mutual trust between you and the person who does this for you.

Living without credit can be a very positive discipline to develop. There is no feeling like being debt free. Most purchases that are financed are completely unnecessary. Even a home or auto bought on time can be needlessly extravagant. You will never be truly free as long as you owe someone else. Pay as you go, live within a budget, and save as much as possible, and in the long run you will be much happier.

If you are going to pay bills while in refuge, use money orders and mail them through your mail drop/remailing service cover. Always save the money order stub, just in case a payment gets lost in the mail. You can use the stub to trace the order and get a refund if it was not cashed.

One drawback to the route Unlucky Larry chose is that his credit has been seriously damaged. He derives some satisfaction from knowing that his wife, who always depended on him financially, is suffering, but he will have to repair his credit rating in the future when he is done adventuring on the trail. He has plenty of cash to tide him over, so he is okay with this.

One last word: whether or not you continue to make payments

on your debts while hidden is up to you. It is extremely unlikely that anyone will find you if you follow the directions in this book. But you do not want a mess waiting for you when you go home. If you can honor your debts while away, then it is best to do so.

MISCELLANEOUS FINANCIAL CONSIDERATIONS

In closing this chapter, there are a few more items that I want to touch on:

- Insurance—especially health coverage. This is a virtual necessity in modern society. If you currently have a policy, then I suggest paying up the premiums through the time you expect to be gone. Yes, you run a discovery risk if you use it in your new area, especially if your plan penalizes you for using doctors outside your "local network." But you also run a risk ignoring physical problems that could be signs of serious illnesses. One possible way around this dilemma is to find a physician in the area you will be in who will take cash payments. I found one in the area I took refuge in that only charged me $25 per visit. He did require me to fill out an initial application asking such embarrassing things as my Social Security number, but, as I recall, my answers on the form were highly inaccurate. You may also find a charity or government clinic that offers free services. Look around. This may be a major factor in determining where you spend your time in exile.
- Skills—there are things you should learn more about for your exodus. First aid techniques are good to know. Carry a good emergency medical kit with you. Take vitamins, exercise, and try to avoid stress. I advise against carrying a weapon, especially a handgun. But a knowledge of self-defense, both unarmed and/or using unconventional weapons like sticks, could save your life. Loompanics and Paladin Press sell dozens of books on first aid and self-defense. A good wilderness survival manual could come in handy too, in case the dung really hits the fan.

- Utilities—call to have them shut off if you have them in your name. Have any deposits forwarded to you through your mail drop system. Try not to cash the check while you are on "sabbatical."
- Red herrings—I strongly suggest that you leave behind false "clues" as to your whereabouts. For example, if you are headed for Montana, get the Florida Department of Tourism to send you stacks of pamphlets about vacationing on their sunny beaches. Leave these in places where those wondering about you will find them. Right before you leave, you may want to mention to a few gossipy types that you have always wanted to see Alaska, knowing the whole time that Arizona is your destination.
- The pseudocide solution—this is a drastic way of discouraging pursuers, but it may be necessary to keep others from coming after you. Go to the ocean front or to the steep banks of a very wide, deep river, and leave a set of your identification along with a "suicide" note written by hand, saying something to the effect of "this was the only way out." Leave some clothes, too, in a place where someone is likely to find them—preferably lifeguards or others in authority. This will scare the hell out of anyone who cares about you, but it is also very likely to shake anyone off your trail. Consider it as a last option if your situation warrants it (e.g., a homicidal spouse is trying to track you down to kill you).

In the next chapter we will discuss how to actually make the big break. Read on, fellow privacy seekers, read on.

4

Means of Escape

Alrighty then. You've got your gear stashed, a wad of cash on you, and you're ready to roll. But what is the best way out of town?

There are a number of op-tions—specifically buses, trains, and planes, as well as your own feet.

BUSES

When it comes to economy, nothing beats the bus for trans-portation. I am not referring here to city transit systems but to the large private carrier in the United States, Greyhound Bus Lines. According to its Web site (www.greyhound.com), the cost of a round-trip ticket from Atlanta to L.A. at the time of this writing (summer 2002) is less than $200. That's without taking discounts into account. If I were a senior citizen or college student or I wanted to buy several days in advance, the rate would be even cheaper. Greyhound goes virtually everywhere in the United States and even has connections into Canada.

I used to ride Greyhound quite a bit in the '80s and early '90s, and my experience was not always good. In those days the buses were cramped and passengers were packed in like sardines. Drivers were generally rude, and fellow travelers were often mental patients or criminal thugs. Sleeping was possible if you were not sitting next to someone. If you were, it was a constant struggle to keep from drifting off and having your head hit his or her shoulder. This is why frequent bus riders often look like sleep-deprived zombies in a perpetual state of stupor.

The bus has a bathroom of sorts. It is like one of those porta-potties they set up at county fairs and construction sites. There is only one on the bus, so you may be waiting a while to use it. It is usually smelly, dirty, and out of toilet paper. Smoking is now illegal on the bus, so smokers will go to the toilet to sneak a few puffs. The smell makes it hard on us nonsmokers.

The newer buses are supposed to be roomier than the old ones, according to Greyhound's Web site. Traveling this way can be fun if the bus is not too crowded. You can stretch out across the seats next to you when they are empty and get some decent sleep. Be sure to bring a blanket and pillow if you will be riding overnight, along with your own toilet paper.

The bus will make periodic stops where you can get off, stretch your legs, use a real toilet, and get a meal. I advise carrying your own food; the restaurants in bus stops are often horrible. I ate at one in Knoxville, Tennessee, one time. The fried chicken was nothing but burnt, blackened skin stuck to the bones. Try to avoid going outside the bus stop while on layover, especially if you are in a larger city. They tend to be in the bad parts of town.

All in all, the bus is not a bad way to go if you will be traveling for a day or less. Try to ride during daylight hours only. And don't eat the fried chicken. Sally and Working Man Jack took the bus, were only on it a few hours during the day, and are none the worse for wear.

TRAINS

A much more pleasant way to travel is by train. By this I mean Amtrak, the privately owned but heavily subsidized passenger rail company that serves the United States. Amtrak is everything that Greyhound is not. The seats are spacious and comfortable. The passengers are generally middle to upper middle class and, for the most part, are friendly and safe. Private sleeping rooms are available at additional cost if you don't want to ride coach.

Bathrooms are abundant on the train. They have regular flush toilets that empty into a holding tank on the bottom of the train. (Sometimes the older ones would dump the waste directly on the tracks. I rode these when I was in college in the '80s. It was fun to watch the hole open up and spill the fruits of my labors on the rail ties as the train sped by.) Bathrooms in private cars usually have showers.

The train will have a restaurant featuring tasty, wholesome food and a lounge car where you can get a drink or snack and watch the world pass by outside. Trains west of the Mississippi have double-decker lounge cars. The view from the top level of these is incredible. Many people love traveling by train, myself included.

The train is not cheap. I just checked the fare from Atlanta to Los Angeles, riding coach with no upgrades. It was more than $800 round trip, four times the cost of Greyhound. If you plan to use one of these services, I recommend you weigh savings versus trip quality and judge accordingly. You can visit Amtrak on the Web at www.amtrak.com. There are various discounts available at different times; these can reduce the cost of the ticket greatly.

PLANES

There is also the option of taking a plane where you are going. I can tell you little about this because I hate to fly. I do know that buying your ticket well in advance will allow you to get a better fare, and I list some Web sites in the appendices that can help you get a cheaper ticket. For anonymity's sake, buy your ticket with a prepaid charge card that has the Mastercard or Visa logo on it, and have the ticket mailed to an address besides your own. Prepaid charge cards work just like regular or secured credit cards, except they can be purchased without credit references, proof of employment or residence, or even identification. You can buy them at many drug stores or other retailers, including AAA Travel. Visit the Web site www.wiredplastic.com to learn more.

YOUR FEET

Are you broke? If you are healthy, then there is a way of getting to where you are going absolutely free: walk. Have fun. Unlucky Larry took this route. He is walking to Maine, his vehicle abandoned in a small town he hitchhiked from to get to the beginning of the Appalachian Trail.

I discussed hitchhiking in an earlier chapter. Those serious about thumbing it should read The Hitchhiker's Handbook from Loompanics. If you already own a vehicle, then you may be tempted to use it to get you where you are going. I advise against this for a few reasons. The most important one is that your car or truck is tied to you by registration, tags, insurance, and so on. If you get a ticket or have an accident while away from home, then it will show up on your driving record. Any investigator, amateur or pro, will find the information and know where you are.

Also, the authorities in most locales take a dim view of people running around in their area with out-of-state plates. If your refuge is in another state, you will probably be required to switch registration and driver's licenses within 90 days or less of arriving (depending on the state). If you do so, your records will connect, leading a path right to you. Oh, hello, honey. What a big gun you have. How did you find me?

Having said all this, I realize that many people may have no option but to use their own vehicle to escape. I did so, in fact, and had no problems. If you do, I make the following recommendations:

- Pay your insurance and registration up for as long into the future as you can before you take off, preferably for an entire year. You don't want them expiring while you are away.
- Slow down! Drive in a careful and courteous manner while in refuge. This is always good advice, but is doubly important when you are trying not to be found. Remove any bumper stickers. It does not pay to ride around New York City flaunting a "Go Braves!" logo.
- Drive as little as possible, and if possible take different routes to the same locations, such as work and shopping. You don't want the local fuzz seeing that out-of-state tag speed past them at the same spot every day week after week.
- It helps to live in a college town if you bring your car. The police are used to vehicles from all over. Get a college decal for your car if you can. This will help allay any suspicions.
- Special note to those driving a vehicle in danger of repossession—it is important that you not keep your vehicle at an address the repo man might check. If you are staying with a relative, you are at high risk of losing your wheels if you park at this person's home. This is true whether or not the relative was listed on your credit application. Skip tracers will always suspect you are staying with family and will aim their investigations accordingly. Park well away from your relative's home. If there is a garage, you can try locking your vehicle in there at night. But be on the lookout for vehicles shadowing you. If the repo man finds out where you are staying, he may very well stake you out. The farther you are geographically from your old digs, the safer you are. If you are worried about repossession, I highly recommend that you read Repossession: Both Sides of the Story from Loompanics. It offers solid strategies for foiling

repossession agents. As mentioned before, repossession agents are extremely effective and ruthless in their methods, but they can be thwarted if you leave absolutely no trail to your refuge.

If you are still in the same state, you can buy another car when you arrive at your refuge. You can drive on the dealer's tag for a while, and there will be no need to get a new license. This will require significant funds, of course.

WHAT TO BRING REVISITED

I touched earlier on what to bring with you, and I want to revisit that now. Make sure you are familiar with the climate of the place you are going. I drove cross-country from Georgia to Washington in July one time. I figured that, since I was traveling during the hottest month of the year, I would have no need for warm clothing. Wrong! When I got to the Pacific Northwest it was freezing. Eastern Washington state can be a very cold, lonely place in July, especially at night. So can the Olympic National Forest. So learn from my mistake and check out the local climate before you pack.

There are products sold in certain regions of the country that are nearly impossible to find in others. For example, headache powders are sold throughout the South but are unknown in the Northeast. Since these are the only things I have found that can tame my headaches, I took a very large supply with me for my trip. You may be addicted to grits, Drake's Coffee Cakes, or some other item peculiar to your area. Still pack light, but take along some of these things if you can. They will help you feel less homesick.

Don't carry fancy luggage that will catch a thief's eye. Old, battered suitcases are good, as are military-style duffel bags. Backpacks will work. Be aware that airlines are particular about what kinds of baggage they will allow on their planes. If you use a backpack, make sure it is airline approved.

By the way, who the hell are you? Are you sure you know? Whether you are or not, the subject of fake ID is one we should address.

FAKE ID

You may or may not have use for fraudulent identification, depending on your situation. It can come in handy when checking into a motel or campground if you are worried about there being a record of your staying there. If you are going to be working in your new locale, I believe that a new Social Security card with a number other than yours can be useful. I am not advising you to do anything illegal, of course.

Be aware that false identification has serious limits. Never try to fool the cops with it! There are different types of fraudulent ID. So-called "foundation documents" are used to establish identity. The most common of these are state-issued driver's licenses or ID cards and the Social Security card. Identification can be purchased from a variety of mail order companies, or, if you are good with computers, there are programs you can use to make your own. I list sources in the back for further research.

Okay! Your trip has gone well, and you have arrived at your place of refuge. Now let's talk about the first few days and what you should do.

SETTLING IN

If your situation allows, you should relax a little and get your bearings. You have probably been through a bit of emotional turmoil, though you may have been too busy to be aware of it. A good night's sleep and a hearty meal can do wonders.

Unless you decided to try one of the more nomadic options I described, you are probably going to be spending most of your time in the same general area. Get to know it a little. Find the grocery store, the pharmacy, the department or variety store, and the gas station, if you have a vehicle.

You want to establish a mail drop as soon as possible. Again, I advise using a private service instead of the U.S. Postal Service. Have the drop you established in your old location forward the mail to the new one. You should have no worries.

When dealing with the locals, be friendly but discreet. I must disagree with other writers on new identity subjects who advise strongly against relocating to a small town. Little communities and rural areas tend to be safer and much cheaper to live in than large cities. Dress like the average Joe or Jane, have some bland cover story to explain your presence, and everything should go fine.

Once you are settled in, you will probably want to start making money.

5

Making Money

Unless you have sufficient funds to take care of yourself or have another means of support, your best option for earning cash in your new location will probably be a good, old-fashioned thing called a "job." If you need to get to work right away, I highly recommend temporary employment agencies, since you are only going to be there temporarily. "Temping" can be a fun way to make a living. I have worked for several agencies over the years, and most of my experiences have been positive ones. Look in the Yellow Pages for a listing of agencies under "Employment," and set up appointments to visit several of them.

The agency will have you fill out one of its applications, give you a brief interview, and probably give you some basic employment tests. These are not hard for anyone of average intelligence to do well on. They are usually meant to measure your command of basic English and simple arithmetic. If you want to work in an office, the staff may give you a typing test as well as quiz you on your computer skills. Usually a working knowledge of Microsoft Windows is all they want.

References can be a challenge. It is important that you not list real places you worked; if the agency calls them your cover is blown. You should create a fictional work history that closely represents your actual level of skills, experience, and knowledge. Screeners can spot a resumé that greatly exaggerates an applicant's past achievements. Don't apply for a position you are not sure you can handle.

It used to be that agencies rarely checked references, but since the tragic events of September 11, 2001, they are being more diligent, especially if you are applying for office work. Applicants for blue-collar positions are not checked as thoroughly, especially if the work is of an unskilled nature. If you are trying to get a white-collar job, I suggest lying on your application and/or resumé, and, if possible, setting up a false reference to back up your deceit. This can be done in a couple of ways.

You can hire a secretarial/answering service to answer the phone in the name of a business you make up. The person from the agency will call the number you provide and state that he or she is trying to confirm your employment. The service will take a message and say that you will return the call. You or a confederate then call the agency back, pretending to be your "old" boss. Better be sure you are good at disguising your voice if you are the one who calls! Your "old boss" confirms the information you put on the application and says some positive things about what a good worker you were (don't overdo it; this can arouse suspicions).

Another way of handling this is to have your "old boss" fax a letter of recommendation to the agency. Most remailing services will receive and forward faxes for you. Tell the agency that your old employer is hard to catch because of time constraints or whatever. Then inform them that you have his home number, but he gave it to you for emergencies only, so you cannot give it to them. But you will call him and have him fax a confirmation/recommendation letter to them.

You then write your own letter, which will look something like this:

Fax it to your remailing service in your own town, and have them fax it to the agency where you applied for work. To make this as simple as possible, you want your false résumé/applica-

---

I.R. Bullshitter
Sticky Widget Corporation
213 Snookered Lane
Lowdown, KS 00000
March 22, 2002

To Whom It May Concern;

 I recently received an inquiry from your firm about a former employer of ours, Mr. Joe Fakename. Mr. Fakename was employed by our company from January 3, 1992 until December 1, 2001 as an account auditor. His employment record with us was superlative, and he was noted several times for the quality of his work, his attendance, and his good attitude. I recommend him to you without reservation. Should I be able to help further, feel free to call. I am difficult to reach at times due to my schedule, but will respond as soon as possible.

Most Truly Yours,

I.R. Bullshitter

I.R. Bullshitter
President, Sticky Widget Corporation

tion data to say that you have worked at this same company for the past several years—the longer the better. The agency will love this. Be sure to apply at several different agencies to maximize your chances of being offered work. You should have employment soon.

These agencies pay by the week, and some offer health insurance and other benefits. You will need a phone number to give them. If nothing else, a phone number for a prepaid cellular phone will do.

When I was in refuge, I worked for an agency and had a very good time. I worked as a temp in a company's sales department to get them through their busy season. I was paid a good hourly wage as well as commissions on my sales. A silver tongue can come in handy with opportunities like these. By the way, that is a very flattering outfit you have on.

You may want to use a bogus Social Security number while you work during your refuge. I did not and had no problems. The Social Security Administration and IRS will know where you really are, but unless your pursuers can access those databases (highly unlikely), then you will be fine. If this still concerns you, then it is possible to work for several months with an incorrect number. I do not advise it, but you may feel it is best. Refer to Appendix III in the back of the book to see how Social Security numbers are assigned. You are on your own with this.

There are ways of obtaining a new number, but they are beyond the scope of this book. If you ever decide to disappear permanently, this will be something you'll need to investigate. I have been told it can be rather challenging, especially in these paranoid post-9/11 days.

You might have to settle for less-than-ideal employment while in refuge. Some jobs are easier to get than others. Telephone work (telemarketing, phone surveys, customer service) is extremely easy to find. Nobody wants to do these jobs. If you have a good speaking voice and know how to handle people, then telemarketing can be a lucrative field. Most people are not overtly rude to you; they just hang up or say "no thanks" if they are not interested in your pitch. Bill collecting is another type of phone work that is easy to get and pays fairly well. You have to be something of an asshole to do well at this.

Janitorial, food service, and manual labor are all honest professions that need workers desperately. Convenience store clerks and security guards are in demand nationwide. You need to find out whether your employer will require a background check for these jobs. In many states, security workers are required to submit to extensive criminal records and other checks. Find out before you apply; even if your past is squeaky clean, the check itself can create a data trail right to you.

I worked as a guard for well over a year, and most of the time I was getting paid to read books and listen to the radio. Third shift positions can be very laid back. If your relief doesn't show up when your shift is over, you are obliged to stay on duty until someone shows up to take over. This can be a good chance for overtime pay.

Maybe you are planning to be a nomad during your refuge, or perhaps you insist on being self-employed. There are ways to accommodate you. Virtually every town of any size has a corner where unemployed men gather early in the morning to try to obtain a day's work. You can join them and probably find a position. Construction company owners will ride by and offer you a day's work doing some sort of labor. You might be picking produce, cleaning up a work site, or whatever. Generally these deals pay cash at the end of the day. Working Man Jack did this for the first few days to get some immediate cash and to meet the owners of some of the local construction companies. He soon had a regular job with a local company, making a good hourly wage.

If you do work for yourself, painting and lawn work gigs are easiest to get. You can put an ad in the paper or just go door to door offering your services. Work for cash only if possible. Use your imagination to find work. Even collecting aluminum cans on the side of the road for recycling pays some money.

These days, it is vital that you have a marketable job skill if you don't want to empty trash cans or flip burgers the rest of your days. There may be a vocational school nearby that you can attend; if not, there are many good correspondence schools that teach computer programming, small engine repair, floral design, and dozens of other good skills. Make sure the one you use is reputable. Consult the Web site www.detc.org for a listing of schools that are nationally accredited and have good reputations.

Work hard and keep a good attitude and you will be successful. America is still a land of opportunity, despite the best efforts of the politicians.

Everyone knows that all work and no play makes one a dull boy, so let's look at the lighter side of taking a powder.

6

Recreation and Fun

I strongly warn against getting your fun from alcohol or drugs. These substances can affect your judgment and give you loose lips. Remember, it is best to be discreet in your dealings with others in your place of refuge. Be friendly, but don't expect to make any real, long-term friends. This was a lesson that Working Man Jack and Sally had to learn; they both enjoy having a good time. The folks who run Sally's shelter are very good at keeping tabs on her, so she has little opportunity to party.

If you took my advice about locating near a college town, then you should have no trouble finding entertainment at a reasonable price, especially if you like live music. These communities often have a very casual atmosphere and lots of transients. They are fun to hang out in. Libraries and parks are free or cost practically nothing to use. Exercising your brain as well as your body costs almost nothing, and the benefits are enormous.

If you are spiritually minded, don't neglect this part of your life while in refuge. It may be necessary to exercise just a bit of discretion in attending services, though, especially if the ministers of your faith are under common authority or otherwise linked. You do not want your new pastor, priest, rabbi, or guru talking to the one back home and finding out who you are; well-meaning people can inadvertently blow your cover or even put you in danger. Maybe switching to another denomination temporarily is best if your beliefs permit this.

In general, you want to live a quiet, peaceable life while in your "disappearance" phase. Avoid publicity, avoid trouble, and behave yourself, and all will be well. Remember to have a bland, believable cover story and stick to it. If things get tough at times, remind yourself that your exile is only temporary. (In fact, you may like your "new life" so much that you decide to make it permanent. More on that in the next chapter.)

Above all, I urge you to make it a time of reflection and self-examination. Try to take stock of your life up to the present. Look for ways to avoid the troubles that caused you to take off in the first place. Otherwise, you may find yourself back in the same boat.

As a book that can teach you better living skills as well as help you financially and spiritually, I give my highest recommendation to the Paladin Press book Living Well on Practically Nothing by Edward H. Romney. It is full of tips on how to live well without spending a fortune, and it is a fascinating and inspiring read at the same time. You will find it on Paladin's Web site at www.paladin-press.com.

Good luck, and God be with you.

7

Wrapping Things Up

To every journey there needs be an end. As this book is about getting away for a while without a trace, it is logical that we conclude with a discussion about returning to your old haunts. Of course, there will be those who have no desire to return, and I will address that as well.

When and if you decide to return home, you will need to settle any affairs in the place where you have taken refuge. If you have been sheltered or otherwise aided by others, you should at least thank them for their kind assistance, and possibly offer them a gift or other compensation for their help. Never burn your bridges behind you; you never know when you may need to cross them again.

If you have been working a job, then you should turn in a notice if possible. Sometimes doing so will prompt your employer to tell you to forget the notice and take a hike immediately. If you think this may be the case, then just leave them high and dry. Assholes like that deserve what they get. Working Man Jack had a great experience with the company he was with, so he turned in a full two weeks notice. Now he has a good reference he can use to find work back home.

If you have been self-employed, let your clients know that your services will soon no longer be offered. Don't leave customers in the lurch. Remember what I said about not burning bridges behind you. If nothing else, they may serve as valuable references when you open up shop back home.

Now is the time to see any sights you have been putting off seeing and to gather a few souvenirs of your little adventure. Do NOT, however, lower your guard and start blabbing about your real reasons for being in the area. And don't start acting up at the end. Stupid mistakes like these can come back to bite you in the butt. Make your exit with class and discretion.

RE-EMERGING

It makes no sense to return to your old life if the problems that led you to seek sanctuary are still active. Make sure the finance company is satisfied, the stalker is in prison, or the problem is otherwise resolved before you head home. Still keep your communications discreet, though.

Sally was able to catch a bus home to testify against her old love. He got 20 years with no chance of parole, and she is now safe. She is taking computer courses at the local vocational college and will soon have a high-paying and secure job.

If you left behind family or friends you did not share your plans with, then they may be a little pissed when you show up after they have written you off as dead. There are two options for dealing with this:

1. Simply tell them the truth. This is the easiest and often the best approach. Once they understand that you were facing a major crisis, they will likely be understanding and just glad that you are safe. Sally did this, as did Working Man Jack. Their friends and family were just glad to have them back.
2. Lie. Being a mischievous type, this was my approach. I have been telling inquirers that I was driving down a lonely country road on a dark evening last fall when a glowing, saucer-shaped object appeared in the air. Suddenly short, grayish beings with huge heads were standing in the road in front of me as my engine stalled. The next thing I knew it was Summer of 2002, and I was lying naked in a field with mysterious bruises all over my body and an anus that was swollen like hell. That's all I know, honest.

You may have a financial mess on your hands when you get back if you did not keep up with your bills. Try to contact your creditors and set up a payment plan. A debt counseling organization may be of some help, as might the various books available on credit repair, such as BestCredit: How to Win the Credit Game (Paladin Press).

Of course, after being away for a while, you may just want to say to hell with it all and stay gone.

SAYING TO HELL WITH IT ALL

There are many possible reasons for staying gone. You may not have realized until you took off just how shitty your old life was. You may have concluded that the problems back home either can't be solved or aren't worth the effort. Or you may have fallen in love with your new life and decided to make it permanent. Whatever the reason, there are things you must consider.

Permanent identity change is possible, even in the age of Big Brother. You must realize that there are only three identifiers that allow the government and private sources to keep tabs on you. These are your name, your birth date, and your Social Security number. Alter these and you will literally appear to slip between

**Having returned home, the author celebrates
in high style with friends and family.**

the cracks, as far as the major databases are concerned. You can then acquire new identifiers and re-emerge for all practical purposes reborn, your old life left behind forever. With care and caution it is possible to avoid any past mistakes you have made and do well in your new identity. You must always exercise some degree of caution to maintain a low profile lest you are discovered, however.

The most difficult identifier to alter is your Social Security number, but it can be done. If you are considering this, I highly recommend that you read the most up-to-date books you can find on permanent ID change. The two currently on the market that I think are the best are How to Disappear in America and The Paper Trip III, both published by Eden Press, and Modern Identity Changer, published by Paladin Press. (By the way, Unlucky Larry did this, and he is now Lucky Larry, working under his new name of Rusty Shackelford at an outdoors store in Colorado, where the possibilities for outdoor recreation are endless. His wife was not so lucky; she choked on a stale pastry she bought to console herself after her boyfriend dumped her.)

There is a method of identity change I recently read about that seems more foolproof than others. You find someone who is dying of AIDS or another incurable disease and arrange to "take over" their life in exchange for monetary compensation. Since death certificates are normally only filed in the county in which the death occurs, you must not reside in that county. Other than that limitation, this technique seems quite sound.

After nine months in refuge, I can honestly say that my life is much better. I have been able to take stock of things to realize how much I have been under the control of false guilt and incorrect thinking. I have seen new things, met new people, and learned new skills. I am a better person for the experience. I sincerely hope that your "sabbatical" will be just as rewarding for you. I wish you all the best.

As a final note, I want to announce a little contest. I have dropped little hints throughout this book about what state I took refuge in but never actually said which one it was. I am interested in learning how many of my faithful readers can figure it out. So I make the following offer: if you think you know where I was, then write to me in care of the publisher and tell me the state and why you came to your conclusion. The first five readers who guess correctly will receive a free, autographed copy of this book.

Again, best of luck to all of you. Take care.

I

Resources for Abused Women

It is a tragedy that we live in a society where violence against women is all too common. Those seeking to escape abusers have a variety of options, fortunately. The first step is to discreetly contact local law enforcement, who can advise you of your options. Either they or the local welfare agency will be able to refer you to shelter resources in your area. By the same token, contacting law enforcement, social services, and churches in the area where you plan to seek refuge can be fruitful as well. I offer the following contacts for additional study:

Advocates for Battered Women
www.aristotle.net/~abw/abwhist.htm
Assists with shelter, counseling, and support.

Batteredwomen.com
www.batteredwomen.com
A resource to help victims gather information, get help, and realize they are not alone. Includes a state-by-state list of hotlines.

Southern California Coalition for Battered Women
www.sccbw.org
Help for women in California.

Erickson Mediation
www.ericksonmediation.com
Legal and other assistance; many links to other resources.

National Domestic Violence Hotline
800-799-7233

Women Against Domestic Violence, Inc.
www.wadv.com
A group of survivors dedicated to stopping domestic violence through communication and support. This site includes links to a variety of resources.

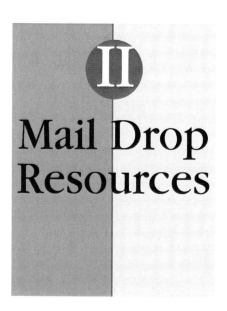

Mail Drop Resources

www.bnl.com
Lists more than 9,000 mail for-warding services in the United States.

www.mbe.com
Official Web site for Mailboxes Etc., a national chain of mail forwarding services with more than 3,000 locations.

The Eden Guide to Private Mail Drops
Eden Press
P.O. Box 8410
Fountain Valley, CA 92728
www.edenpress.com
With this book you can find a mail drop almost anywhere in the world. It lists more than 3,000 in

the United States, as well as more than 400 in 90 foreign countries.

II

How Social Security Numbers Work

These numbers are assigned by the Social Security Administration. If you want to use a bogus number, then you must understand how they are organized. The first three numbers correspond to the state you were born in. They have been assigned as follows:

001-003 — New Hampshire
004-007 — Maine
008-009 — Vermont
010-034 — Massachusetts
035-039 — Rhode Island
040-049 — Connecticut
050-134 — New York
135-158 — New Jersey
159-211 — Pennsylvania
212-220 — Maryland
221-222 — Delaware

223-231 — Virginia
232-236 — West Virginia
237-246 — North Carolina
247-251 — South Carolina
252-260 — Georgia
261-267 — Florida
268-302 — Ohio
303-317 — Indiana
318-361 — Illinois
362-386 — Michigan
387-399 — Wisconsin
400-407 — Kentucky
408-415 — Tennessee
416-424 — Alabama
425-428 — Mississippi
429-432 — Arkansas
433-439 — Louisiana
440-448 — Oklahoma
449-467 — Texas
468-477 — Minnesota
478-485 — Iowa
486-500 — Missouri
501-502 — North Dakota
503-504 — South Dakota
505-508 — Nebraska
509-515 — Kansas
516-517 — Montana
518-519 — Idaho
520 — Wyoming
521-524 — Colorado
525 — New Mexico
526-527 — Arizona
528-529 — Utah
530 — Nevada
531-539 — Washington
540-544 — Oregon
545-573 — California

574 — Alaska
575-576 — Hawaii
577-579 — Washington, D.C.

You must make sure that the first three digits of the number you are using correspond with the state you are from (or are claiming to be from). The second set of (two) numbers (000-00-0000) can be selected at random. The last four digits are random serial numbers, which could be anything from 0000 to 0009, but try to mix the numbers up (e.g., 3986, not 1234 or 5555).

You can work for several months under a bogus number, but eventually your employer will be notified. You can then supply another false number (or your real one, as I did without any resulting problems), apologizing for your carelessness, or just move on to other employment. In any event, the Social Security number is not an insurmountable problem for the seeker of sanctuary. I worked under my real number for nine months with no difficulties.

IV

Resources for Further Study

The following works and Internet links are in addition to the ones mentioned in the text. They may be helpful, depending on your situation:

Web Sites for Publishers of Privacy, New ID, and Survival Material

www.paladin-press.com
Paladin Press

www.deltapress.com
Delta Press

www.edenpress.com
Eden Press

Books

Advanced Fugitive: Running, Hiding,
Surviving, and Thriving *Forever*
By Kenn Abaygo
Paladin Press
Boulder, CO
Learn the techniques real fugitives have used to evade dedicated pursuers.

The Complete Idiot's Guide to Camping and Hiking
By Michael Mouland
Alpha Books, an imprint of Pearson Education
New York, NY
If you have never set foot in the outdoors before, or if you are contemplating going backpacking or car camping during your sabbatical, then this book is a good place to start.

How to Make Driver's Licenses and
Other ID on Your Home Computer
By Max Forge
Loompanics Unlimited
Port Townsend, WA
Explains how to make your own ID on a personal computer instead of ordering a set.

How to Spot a Phony Resumé: The Management Advantage
By Wayne D. Ford, Ph.D.
Management Advantage Inc.
Walnut Creek, CA
Shows the most common mistakes individuals make in synthesizing information on their resumé. It will show you what NOT to do.

The Last Frontiers on Earth: Strange
Places Where You Can Live Free
By Jon Fisher
Loompanics Unlimited
Port Townsend, WA
Covers possible retreat locales, including living on a boat, as a nomad, in ghost towns, on an ice cap, in a secret cellar, etc.

Modern Survival Retreat
By Ragnar Benson
Paladin Press
Boulder, CO
Designed as an instruction manual for soldiers trying to avoid capture, this book contains useful information for those wishing to evade detection.

The Safe House
By Jefferson Mack
Paladin Press
Boulder, CO
Explains how these sanctuaries work, how to find them, and how to set one up.